Original title:
Tales from Titan

Copyright © 2025 Creative Arts Management OÜ
All rights reserved.

Author: Franklin Stone
ISBN HARDBACK: 978-1-80567-818-2
ISBN PAPERBACK: 978-1-80567-939-4

Journey into the Abyssal Night

In a rocket made of cheese, we soar,
Sipping ice cream through space's galore.
With penguins in space suits, we prance,
Dancing with comets, oh what a chance!

The stars giggle as we float by,
A banana split moon makes us sigh.
Asteroids cry out, 'Don't crash, please!'
While aliens juggle their flying unease.

Through rings of Saturn, we twist and spin,
Catching stardust that tickles our chin.
Cosmic popcorn pops loud in the night,
As Martians flip pancakes in joyous delight.

With dreams of robots that paint the sky,
We paint our faces with colors high.
The void rolls with laughter, a cosmic party,
A journey delicious, never too hearty!

Murmurs from the Gaseous Abyss

In clouds of gas where giggles roam,
Bubbles pop, they call it home.
With each puff, a story unfolds,
Of creatures dancing, brave and bold.

They float like balloons, with laughter loud,
Chasing their dreams in a swirly cloud.
One lost a wing, but found a hat,
Said, 'I prefer this, how about that?'

Echoes of Celestial Winds

Whispers tease across the night,
Playful gusts that steal your sight.
They tickle stars and spin them round,
In a cosmic dance, they're safely bound.

A nebula sneezes, bright sparks fly,
While comets giggle as they zoom by.
'Watch this trick!' cries a starry friend,
As he tumbles, ready to ascend.

Patterns in the Hydrocarbon Sands

In golden dunes where laughter's made,
A robot built a sandy glade.
Waves of goo, they slip and slide,
As silly critters join the ride.

With each slip, they make a splash,
Their giggles echo, oh, what a bash!
They sculpt a castle, all askew,
Then claim it's art, not just a zoo!

Secrets of the Frigid Horizon

In icy realms with frosty winks,
Where penguins dance and the sunlight blinks.
They've thrown snowballs, a nightly sport,
And carousel rides where the chilly court.

A snowman grins, with a carrot nose,
Telling tales of where the cold wind blows.
He sways and spins, says, 'Join the dance!'
In a winter wonder, they take a chance.

Mythology of the Misty Moons

In the glow of foggy nights,
Giggles dance with twinkling lights.
A jester hops on Saturn's rings,
Whispering jokes to cosmic kings.

Moons chuckle in a plume of haze,
Winking at the sun's bright rays.
Silly shadows do the twist,
Creating laughter in the mist.

The Voyage of the Dreaming Satellite

A satellite set sail to play,
With fluffy clouds along the way.
It made a friend, a runaway star,
Together they giggled, oh, so far!

Through cosmic giggles, they rolled and spun,
Chasing comets, oh what fun!
With each loop, a new joke told,
In the universe, brave and bold.

Legends Sketched in Frost

On icy worlds where frostbugs cheer,
Legends bloom in winter's sphere.
With snowflakes dressed in silly attire,
They dance around a frosty fire.

Each breath a cloud, each laugh a song,
Twisting tales that can't go wrong.
Outlandish stories in frost unfold,
As starlight winks, so brave and bold.

Patterns of Celestial Beings

Beings sketch their dreams up high,
In casual loops that twist and fly.
They laugh and twirl through velvet night,
Creating patterns in pure delight.

With comet tails like silly strings,
They conjure joy in cosmic flings.
Wiggling wildly, without a care,
Carving giggles in the solar air.

The Lament of Solitude in the Void

In silence I float, a lone silver fish,
No company here, just a cosmic wish.
Stars giggle at me, twinkling away,
In this empty expanse, I'm a bright, lonely ray.

The vacuum sings songs of a long-lost bread,
Each bubble of laughter, a thought in my head.
Is that laughter from stars, or my own silly plight?
I'll dance with the comets, till the end of the night.

Ballad of the Subterranean Streams

Deep in the depths, where the shadows reside,
A stream sings a tune that it can't quite decide.
Rocks turn to singers, they wobble and sway,
  Even the moss seems to join in the play.

Fish sporting hats, they bobble and dive,
Claiming a crown, quite eager to thrive.
I twirl with the algae, all giggles and gleam,
What a fine world, at the bottom of dreams!

Echoes in the Lush Abyss

In the forest of whispers, trees dance and prance,
 With echoes of giggles that lead me to chance.
 I follow the giggles, they twist and they whirl,
    Like a playful kitten, or a hopping pearl.

Creatures with hats, and a twinkly gaze,
    Invite me to join their quirky soirée.
We boogie with shadows, and tickle the light,
    In this jolly abyss, everything feels right!

Ethereal Dreams Adrift in Space

Floating 'mid stars, I catch a funny sight,
A cow's moo echoing in the deep night.
It drifts with a rocket, a baffling scheme,
Who knew cows could launch, in a whimsical dream?

The moons giggle softly, as comets parade,
While aliens laugh with their green, glowy spade.
In a dance of delight, we wobble and sway,
In the cosmos, we find humor in play!

Astral Labyrinths of the Ancient Seas

In the depths where starfish play,
A jellyfish starts ballet,
With squids that do the tango,
They spin and twirl, oh what a show!

Crabs wear hats and give a cheer,
While octopuses sip their beer,
The coral reefs all laugh and tease,
As clams crack jokes with perfect ease.

Pathways to the Wandering Horizon

On the path where lost socks go,
The sunbeams dance, the breezes blow,
A squirrel juggles acorns high,
And giggles when a teapot flies.

The clouds decide to play a game,
Where each one wears a funny name,
With ducks on bikes zooming by,
They honk and wave, oh my, oh my!

Enigmas of the Glistening Terrain

On the hills where marshmallows grow,
A raccoon steals a bowl of dough,
With sprinkles on his furry head,
He jumps around, a silly spread.

The rivers flow with lemonade,
While chocolate fountains serenade,
A bear in boots does pirouettes,
As gophers cheer with loud duets.

Hues of Celestial Mysterium

In the twilight where colors blend,
A cat in space begins to bend,
With stars as yarn, she starts to knit,
Creating galaxies, just a bit!

The planets laugh and tease the moon,
As comets play a merry tune,
With laughter echoing through the void,
Cosmic jokes never get old or paranoid.

The Celestial Mosaic Revealed

In the sky, a jigsaw's dream,
Puzzles flying, or so it seems.
Stars play hide and seek at night,
Whispers giggle, delight in flight.

Comets roller skate on air,
Planets twirl, a cosmic fair.
Saturn boasts of its grand rings,
While Mars just hints at funny things.

Nebulas dance with colors bright,
A dazzling, playful starry sight.
Galaxies sip on stardust sours,
As laughter echoes in the hours.

Each constellation, a joke untold,
Stories of wonders, both shy and bold.
The sky's a canvas, wild and free,
With humor trapped in eternity.

Chronicles etched in Ice and Shadow

In icy lands where shadows play,
Giggles echo, come what may.
Snowmen gossip in the frost,
While polar bears munch, no thought lost.

Shadows waltz under the moon,
Chasing krill on a fun-filled tune.
Penguins sport their fancy shoes,
Dancing tales in winter's blues.

Frosty fairies sprinkle cheer,
As rumors swirl of a friendly deer.
The icebergs chuckle, tipsy and grand,
With jokes carved out by winter's hand.

Each flake of snow, a secret told,
Warming hearts when winds turn cold.
With every slide and every glide,
The joy of ice cannot hide.

Requiem for the Forgotten Realms

In realms where giants left their shoes,
Fairies gossip, trading news.
Ghosts wear laughter like a crown,
Haunting hills, a playful clown.

Old wizards in their dusty halls,
Swapping tales between the walls.
Potions bubble, spitting jokes,
While dragons share their favorite hoax.

Lost in forests, they take a stroll,
Singing songs, the wind their soul.
Crickets chirp in perfect tune,
While moonlit paths chuckle at noon.

Each sigh of stone, a laugh long past,
Mysteries float, both slow and fast.
Through echoes and whispers, they reveal,
The joy in tales that time won't steal.

Myths of the Iridescent Horizon

On horizons painted bright and bold,
Myths of laughter gently unfold.
Rainbows tease with colors wide,
While wildflowers wink with pride.

Clouds become a playful fleet,
Traveling with rhythm and beat.
Kites twist tales in the breeze,
As sunbirds chirp with utmost ease.

Each sunset, a canvas of cheer,
Where magic whispers sweet and near.
A horizon of giggles far and wide,
Leads adventurous hearts to ride.

In dreams, they weave through light and space,
Dancing forth with playful grace.
The edge of day holds comic lore,
Where every chuckle opens a door.

A Rhapsody in Cosmic Color

In a world where cows can fly,
And pizzas rain from yonder sky,
The astronauts dance with glee,
On moons made of bright spaghetti.

Jellybeans grow on candy trees,
Aliens sip cosmic teas,
Each star twinkles a silly tune,
As comets race and giggle, too.

Asteroids play hopscotch in space,
While sunbeams organize a race,
The universe spins in joyful rhyme,
With beings who laugh, all the time.

So grab your hats and join the spree,
In this cosmic jamboree,
Where every orbit's a clownish feat,
And the universe dances to a quirky beat.

Fables of the Eternal Wanderers

Once wandered a snail with a great big dream,
To surf on a cosmic beam,
He met a starfish, wise and sly,
Who taught him how to fly.

A comet rode a bicycle slow,
With a rainbow for a tire, you know,
Together they wrote a zany book,
On how to catch clouds with a hook.

A purple worm wore a hat of cheese,
While dancing atop the cosmic breeze,
They sang of planets made of cream,
And beans that sparked a wild dream.

As they twirled and spun in space,
Silly jokes filled every place,
In this wild, eternal quest,
Laughter echoes, never rests.

Escape to the Enchanted Abyss

In depths where giggles swirl and sway,
A fish tells jokes to lighten the day,
Mermaids chuckle, their tails a-flip,
As octopuses do a funny dip.

Crabs have parties on rainbow rocks,
With conch shell speakers and dancing socks,
The seaweed sways to a beat so fine,
While starfish twist in perfect line.

A jellyfish juggles bright blue pearls,
As dolphins dance with twirls and curls,
Inside the abyss, where laughter beams,
Even shadows join in on the dreams.

So dive right in, leave worries behind,
In this realm of fun, unconfined,
Where every wave tells a jest so bright,
And the abyss glows with pure delight.

The Lullaby of the Whispering Winds

The winds began to softly sigh,
As squirrels wore hats and began to fly,
With whispers of secrets, they danced on high,
In a world where even teardrops cry.

A dandelion's wish took form as a kite,
Spinning tales of glee in twilight,
While clouds dressed in pajamas, cozy and round,
Fell into laughter, so sweet and profound.

Each gust a giggle, as breezes unite,
Turning nonsense into sheer delight,
The moon chuckles, a jester of night,
As stars join in the comical fight.

So close your eyes, let the winds play,
With whispers of joy that brighten your day,
In this lullaby of spirited cheer,
Where every laugh conquers all fear.

Sirens of the Shimmering Seas

In waters bright where seaweed sings,
The fish wear hats and dance on strings.
A crab in shades, full of good cheer,
Invites the dolphins for a beer.

With bubbles popping, giggles sound,
As mermaids twirl, their hair unwound.
A whale attempts the latest craze,
But trips and blunders in a daze.

The octopus plays checkers fine,
While seahorses sip salty wine.
Each tide brings laughter to the shore,
They party till the stars implore.

In shimmering seas, the fun won't cease,
As every wave brings more caprice.
With jiggling jellyfish on parade,
The ocean's antics never fade.

Secrets Beneath the Orange Veil

Beneath the glow of orange skies,
A raccoon wears a wise disguise.
With secrets stashed in leafy nooks,
He writes his tales in funny books.

A turtle with a puzzled frown,
Lost his shell while out in town.
He asks a lizard, quick and spry,
To help him find it—oh my, oh my!

The owls gossip, sipping tea,
About the things they think they see.
And every night, the frogs decide,
To join the dance, no need to hide.

Underneath the orange veil,
Adventures spring, they never pale.
With giggles echoing through the trees,
The forest whispers silly pleas.

Violin Melodies Across the Expanse

A rabbit plays a violin,
With every note, the fun begins.
The owls hoot in harmonic cheer,
As fireflies waltz, drawing near.

The moon joins in with a bright grin,
While stars applaud, their sparks akin.
A raccoon dances, twirls around,
With maracas made from acorns found.

The concert grows with every beat,
As squirrels gather, tapping feet.
A cat brings snacks, some fishy fries,
As laughter fills the endless skies.

In joy, they play till break of dawn,
With music swirling, all forlorn.
For in this expanse, all are free,
To laugh, to dance, to just be glee.

Celestial Driftwood Diaries

On driftwood logs that float around,
The otters scribble tales profound.
Their laughter bubbles on the waves,
While wishing luck on tiny knaves.

A starfish types with wiggly arms,
Telling tales of ocean charms.
While crabs critique the latest news,
And debate which shell is best to use.

The pelicans bring snacks that clash,
With sea salt fries and pickle hash.
As gulls squawk jokes from high above,
They urge the waves to dance with love.

In diaries of wood and tides,
Adventures bloom where fun abides.
Each ripple tells a story bold,
In this great sea where laughter's gold.

Resonance of the Starry Veil

In the glow of the cosmos, a cat takes a leap,
Bouncing off rings, into the unknown deep.
Jupiter chuckles, it's his turn to jest,
While Saturn spins tales in a sparkly vest.

Planets gather round with a glimmering grin,
Playing space charades, where do we begin?
Mars tosses a boomerang made of dust,
A game of galactic, oh yes, it's a must!

Asteroids dance like they've lost their way,
Stumbling through stardust, in a chaotic ballet.
Comets roast marshmallows, bright tails on fire,
Laughing together, they never expire.

Then comes the sun, with a radiant frown,
Blasting a joke that turns day upside down.
Galaxies wobble with laughter so loud,
In the boundless expanse, a humorous crowd.

Celestial Murmurs Beneath a Shimmering Dome

Beneath a dome glittering with joyous light,
Asteroids tell stories that take flight at night.
Venus winks slyly, in glittering attire,
While quirky little stars twinkle, never tire.

Mercury slips, doing a slide on the ring,
Asteroids giggle; they join in to swing.
Neptune's tossing glitter like it's a parade,
In laughter, they swirl, in the vast cosmic shade.

In this wild space, chaos becomes a song,
A medley of merriment, where all belong.
Pluto, with charm, juggles moons with flair,
Making the cosmic combine, laughter to share.

Meteors crack up, making wishes, no doubt,
What if they joined a comedic shout-out?
In this celestial sphere, every giggle is grand,
As laughter resounds in the cosmic band.

Whispers of the Shrouded Moon

Under the pale glow of a chuckling orb,
The moon shares whispers that rattle and absorb.
A frog in a spacesuit hops with great glee,
In a concert of crickets, making lighthearted spree.

With shadows that dance, and comets that tease,
Asteroids roll in, playing games with the breeze.
Martians are knitting, a quilt full of stars,
A blanket for laughter, with threads from Mars.

The twilight giggles with each passing beam,
Chasing lost thoughts as they shimmer and gleam.
"Did you hear the one about the earthling's tune?"
"It's out of this world!" roars the shimmering moon.

Twisting and turning in delightful delight,
They frolic through galaxies, brightening the night.
In cosmic camaraderie, the fun never ends,
Together they twinkle, the universe sends.

Secrets Beneath the Orange Veil

Beneath an orange veil, where laughter erupts,
Aliens share jokes with mischievous pups.
Saturn's rings jangle like a set of chimes,
Creating a rhythm, tickling all in their primes.

While NASA stares up, trying hard to find,
The quirky surprises that float through the mind.
Uranus takes selfies, posing with glee,
'Check my new caption, who's funny as me?'

Bubbles of laughter from Martian balloons,
Floating around, like quirky cartoons.
A cosmic parade filled with whimsical sights,
As stars trade their punchlines on brand new nights.

In the depths of space, where silliness reigns,
Gravity laughs and the universe gains.
Together they twirl, these celestial clowns,
In a colorful burst, without any frowns.

The Cradle of Alien Whispers

In a field where odd things grow,
Little creatures dance with woe.
They trip on roots and crack a grin,
Singing songs of where they've been.

A spaceship lands, a clown hops out,
Shouting tales that make us shout.
With juggling stars and squeaky toys,
They spread laughter, oh what joys!

The wind it laughs, a giggling gale,
As aliens tell of their grand tale.
A game of tag with cosmic rays,
In this place where humor plays.

So if you hear a jolly cheer,
Just know that friends from space are near.
In the cradle where whispers flow,
Laughter echoes, watch it grow!

Chronicles of Echoing Silence

In a valley thick with silence wide,
A duck quacks loudly, hopes to glide.
But echoes bounce with a silly twist,
Taunting the duck, it can't resist.

Passengers from stars above,
Join the fun, fall in love.
They whisper secrets to the shade,
While shadows dance, the game is played.

The echoes giggle, rush and swirl,
One alien's hat gave quite a twirl.
Agitated air, a boisterous sound,
Makes us grin, all around!

So when you walk through quiet lands,
And hear the laughter that expands,
Just know it's friends in spaceships bright,
Crafting tales with sheer delight!

Reflections on Liquid Mirrors

On a lake that shines like funny glass,
Fish wear hats as they all amass.
They peek and pout with silly looks,
Swapping jokes like comic books.

A splash of laughter makes the waves,
And goofy boats, oh how they behave!
With squeaky oars and wobbly sails,
They tell their fishy, funny tales.

Aliens float, in boats so bright,
Casting shadows that dance at night.
They juggle moons, both small and swell,
Leaving ripples, a quirky spell.

So if you find a crazy lake,
With fish that laugh and bounce awake,
Just take a dive, join the cheer,
For in this place, fun's always near!

The Ballad of the Endless Dunes

In sands so vast, a lizard sings,
With floppy ears and golden wings.
He twirls around in a merry spree,
Telling tales of a sunny spree.

A tumbleweed rolls on by,
Chasing shadows, oh my, oh my!
With each turn, it sings a tune,
Of little critters and summer's boon.

Aliens ride on camels tall,
With goofy hats, they laugh and call.
They've lost their way, but they don't care,
For in each laugh, there's joy to share.

So follow the sounds past shifting sands,
And join the fun where laughter stands.
In endless dunes where memories bloom,
Their ballad rolls, dispelling gloom!

Legends Written in Icy Light

In frozen lands where penguins roam,
A walrus claims the ice his home.
He tells tall tales with blubbery glee,
Of snowball fights and a lost cup of tea.

A snowman danced beneath the stars,
While igloos held karaoke bars.
The seals all cheered, their applause was loud,
As the walrus sang, feeling quite proud.

Then came the night with a slip and slide,
When snowball chaos broke the tide.
The penguins laughed, they couldn't escape,
As they tumbled down in a furry cape.

They settled down as the fun wore thin,
With jolly hearts and tails like fin.
In icy light, their laughter soared,
In the legends written, forever adored.

Cinematic Dreams of Distant Shores

On shores where bubbles rise and pop,
A crab directed a film non-stop.
Starring snails in a slow-motion race,
While seagulls swooped down with elegant grace.

The plot was thick with seaweed drama,
As fish took turns in the grand panorama.
A chorus of clams sang out a tune,
Beneath the light of a silvery moon.

Then came a plot twist, oh what a sight!
A dolphin leaped in, bringing pure delight.
With flips and spins, the crowd went wild,
As waves crashed down, each creature smiled.

Their cinematic dreams flowed free and wide,
With laughter echoing, a joyous tide.
This ocean film will forever beam,
In hearts of creatures chasing a dream.

Parables of the Hollow Sky

In a sky of cotton candy and fluff,
Clouds held debates, but were they tough?
A thunderstorm grumbled, full of sass,
While rainbows giggled, oh what a class!

A sparrow spoke of love from above,
While owls critiqued, showing no love.
In the hollow sky, where creatures might soar,
The stars held secrets, and whispered lore.

A meteor danced as it fell from grace,
Landing too hard, oh what a disgrace!
Yet, the moon winked, "Don't take it to heart,
We're all just stardust playing our part."

So they gathered, each tale to share,
With chuckles and quirks floating through air.
In a hollow sky, laughter shines bright,
Uniting all in a whimsical flight.

Reflections of a Deceptive Peace

In a tranquil pond where frogs do croak,
A fish told jokes while catching smoke.
The turtles yawned, quite out of the zone,
While dragonflies danced on their mobile phone.

A beaver hummed of easy days,
As squirrels plotted sneaky plays.
The ducks quacked out their calm refrain,
Not knowing trouble brewed on the plain.

Then came a splash, oh what a sight,
The turtles jumped, it was pure delight!
As ripples spread, the jokes turned quick,
Frogs leapt away, avoiding the trick.

But peace returned, like a warmly worn sock,
As everyone gathered 'round the old oak clock.
In reflections of laughter, each creature found peace,
In a tale where joy never seems to cease.

The Enchanted Bounty of the Orange Spheres

In a land where oranges fly,
The critters dance and nibble pie.
Their laughter echoes, bright and loud,
As fruity jesters gather 'round.

A squishy feast atop a hill,
With jellied smiles that give a thrill.
The giggling trees sway side to side,
As silly squirrels join the ride.

With orange juice that flows like streams,
And silly hats that burst with dreams.
They paint the sky with jokes galore,
And everyone just begs for more.

A ticklish breeze, a funny sight,
The spheres roll by in pure delight.
In this strange land, they all agree,
Life's sweetest dreams are fruity glee.

Beneath the Celestial Skin

Under cosmic blankets vast and wide,
Funny creatures scurry, full of pride.
With googly eyes and wiggly tails,
They tell their jokes in silly trails.

A starry fish, a moonlit cat,
Disguised in laughter, imagine that!
They play hopscotch on a comet's tail,
While spinning yarns of space's tale.

Beneath the skin of night's embrace,
Giggles bounce through the endless space.
Interstellar puns create a scene,
Where even darkness has its sheen.

In fancy suits made out of light,
These cosmic jesters share the night.
With every joke, they beam and glow,
As laughter spreads in cosmic flow.

Mists of Memory Over Ancient Shores

Along the shores of time's great tide,
Waves of laughter swirl and slide.
Old sandcastles wear funny hats,
As the seagulls joke with chitchat chats.

In golden mists where shadows play,
Wily ghosts dance and sway.
They reminisce of battles lost,
While notorious crabs boast the cost.

With tales of treasure, buried deep,
They trade old jokes that make you weep.
A pirate's grin, a mermaid's laugh,
In every wave, a silly gaffe.

The ancient stones break into song,
As echoes stretch, and stretch along.
In this misty place where giggles soar,
History's made of jokes and more.

The Odyssey of An Icy Blue Heart

In a chilly land with frosty glee,
An icy heart must peep to see.
With snowflakes dancing on his nose,
He cracks a joke that surely glows.

His frozen friends, with smiles so bright,
Sparkle like diamonds in the night.
They skate and giggle on the lake,
With every tumble, joy they make.

A penguin troupe in tuxedo flair,
Prattle jokes with frosty air.
In every flurry, puns reside,
As laughter echoes far and wide.

At the end of this snowy spree,
The icy heart cries, "Look at me!"
With every chuckle, warmth ignites,
Turning winter into fuzzy nights.

Ciphers in the Floating Fog

In fog so thick, I lost my shoe,
A trio of ducks just quacked right through.
They wore tiny hats, all graceful and spry,
Who knew that fog could make fashion fly?

I searched for pi—in a drizzle of dew,
The numbers danced like they knew what to do.
A neighbor's cat barked, quite out of place,
And made me ponder on time and space.

I threw a couple of eggs at a wall,
But all they did was giggle and sprawl.
The fog just laughed—it took my breath,
As numbers vanished, it smiled at death.

So here I sit with ducks and my shoes,
In a world where I can just pick and choose.
The ciphers play on in their feathery wigs,
And I keep walking with shadows and digs.

Banners of the Ether Winds

The banners flap in colors so bright,
They tickle the clouds, what a silly sight.
A pink elephant dances on top of a kite,
While squirrels with sunglasses party all night.

A breeze blows in, with whispers of cheese,
And birds sing backup with the utmost ease.
An owl in a tutu conducts from afar,
While space-time sips tea from a chocolate jar.

The winds weave tales in a funny old way,
As gravity sleeps through the light of day.
A unicorn joins, wearing socks on its feet,
And everyone laughs at this nonsensical feat.

So we twirl and we spin with this cosmic flair,
In a wacky parade, with joy in the air.
The banners of ether, so wild and free,
Make each moment a giggle, a quirky jubilee.

The Elysium of the Farthest Moon

In the farthest moon, where the fluffballs roll,
Jellybeans sprout, and time takes a stroll.
A snail on a scooter, so speedy and deft,
Has declared itself king with a jelly crown left.

The daisies all hum, a sweet little song,
While bunnies start dancing and bouncing along.
I stumbled on clovers that tickled my toes,
And wondered if wizards communed with the crows.

Each night, the stars wear pajamas and wink,
While moonbeams giggle and all colors sync.
A walrus in charge makes odd rules of the game,
"Just be silly or else you'll get the blame!"

So I masque with the fluffballs, let laughter ensue,
On a moon where all dreams are magically true.
The joy of the farthest brings smiles anew,
In this wacky Elysium of cosmic hue.

An Odyssey Through Time and Silence

In silence I wandered, with socks mismatched,
Chased by a turtle who happily scratched.
He offered a riddle; I scratched my own head,
And laughed when he said, "Time's best if it's fed!"

Through corridors filled with tick-tock and squeak,
I met a wise toaster who taught me to speak.
"Bread needs respect," he toasted with flair,
"And waffles just melt if no one is there."

I clinked my thick timepiece against a cold wall,
To echoes of laughter—it started to stall.
A ladybug danced on a map full of swirls,
While squirrels debated the fate of their pearls.

So I meandered on, with chaos divine,
Through an odyssey made of jelly and twine.
The silence spoke volumes in whispers of cheer,
As I lost myself laughing, just wandering here.

Chronicles of the Ether Pioneers

In a land of cold and gloom,
Where the methane bubbles bloom,
Pioneers in space suits bright,
Fumble 'round in giddy flight.

One fell down and took a spin,
His helmet caught a rogue blue fin,
Laughter echoed through the air,
As he spun like he don't care.

With their gadgets, what a sight,
Trying to capture stars at night,
One froze up in a funny pose,
Now he's stuck with a methane nose.

Through the glimmers, quirks abound,
Strange creatures dance around,
With giggles riding on the breeze,
Who knew space could be such a tease?

The Luminous Enigma Awaits

Amidst the fogs of bright delight,
A glowing puzzle shines so bright,
We scratched our heads and took a guess,
What's this wacky light, no less?

Turns out it was a silly sign,
Pointing to a cosmic wine,
A vine-twirled bottle on the way,
'Drink up, it's a party today!'

We spilled some on our shiny suits,
Laughed as it turned into root shoots,
Now flowers bloom from our attire,
And we ride the winds of cosmic fire.

As the stars giggle and twinkle bright,
We toast to this wild, merry night,
With the enigma wrapped as jests,
Turns out, laughter's what we quest!

Dreams Adrift in the Methane Skies

Floating dreams in a hazy haze,
In the ethereal, an odd malaise,
We bounce along on clouds of gas,
Taking turns, hoping none will pass.

One tried to dance, but slipped on mist,
With a whoosh and a plop, oh what a twist!
He ricocheted from a crystal lake,
Then laughed so hard, his gears did shake.

No gravity, yet we all stick tight,
Chasing visions in the glittering light,
Twisting, turning through bizarre dreams,
Like marooned clowns in lunar beams.

As we drift through this comic dance,
In our soapy bubble, we take a chance,
In the methane skies, we find our cheer,
With giggles echoing year after year!

Beneath the Clouded Canopy

Underneath a cloud so fluffy,
Where the creatures act all huffy,
We peek through with glee and doubt,
What oddball shenanigans are about?

A fluffy being sneezed a puff,
Sending everyone tumbling, rough,
We rolled around in a giddy mess,
While it chuckled, oh what excess!

A game of tag, now round we go,
Chasing shadows, what a show,
But who knew they'd melt like ice?
Laughter bursts, oh isn't it nice!

Clouds entwined with a joyous song,
In this whimsy, we all belong,
Underneath the canopy wild,
Space-time tickles every child.

Serenade of the Gas Giant

In the swirling clouds of dreams,
Gas bubbles pop with silly beams.
A stormy dance, oh what a sight,
Jovial thunder in the night.

The blimps go flying by with glee,
Chasing the jesters of the spree.
They twirl and spin in vibrant play,
Floating far from the fray.

With ringlets made of creamy foam,
They sing of adventures far from home.
A merry tune, a cosmic jest,
In the vastness, they find their rest.

So if you hear a wacky sound,
It's frolicsome fun that's come unwound.
In this sky of gas and mirth,
Laughter echoes, giving birth.

Echoes in the Hydrocarbon Sea

Bubbles rise in a thick brown brew,
Sipping tea with a jovial crew.
Creatures dance in the gloopy night,
Wobbling round in sheer delight.

They splash and giggle in the goo,
Chasing waves that look so new.
Blimps of gold and silver fly,
Skimming surface, oh my, oh my.

Each drop sparkles like silly stars,
While they race in their tiny cars.
Laughter ripples through the thick, dark haze,
Making memories in myriad ways.

So join the fun on this slippery shore,
With friends galore, you'll never bore.
In this sea of vibrant cheer,
Silly antics are always near.

Chasing Shadows on the Frozen Surface

On icy plains where shadows creep,
Snowmen giggle, taking a leap.
Juggling snowflakes, what a sight,
In a ballet of frosty delight.

They skate and slide with clumsy style,
Chasing dreams with every mile.
While footloose friends mock their grace,
Silly slips, oh what a race!

In this wintry wonderland so bright,
Snow launches high in a frosty fight.
With laughter echoing all around,
Joy transcends this frosted ground.

So grab your gear and join the trend,
In this icy world, where fun won't end.
For in the cold, warmth is found,
As friendship spins round and round.

Letters to a Distant World

I wrote a letter to the moons,
With funny tales and silly tunes.
They giggled back, oh what a cheer,
Invisible ink, but loud and clear.

I sent them jokes in starry flight,
Delivered fast by cosmic light.
They laughed so hard, they made a wish,
To swim in laughter's endless swish.

Each stamp a dream from the void,
In whimsy's grip, we're all enjoyed.
For every word brings us near,
In this galaxy of glee and cheer.

So if you pen to worlds afar,
Know laughter travels, bright as a star.
In ink of joy, with friendship's twirl,
We pen our hopes to the distant world.

Legends of the Forgotten Void

In a vacuum where laughter rides,
Frogs wear capes, and humor hides.
Asteroids dance, quite out of tune,
While singing chefs bake galactic moon.

Jupiter's moons play hide and seek,
With sneaky smiles, they never speak.
Comets slip, with a giant grin,
Making space dishes spin and spin.

Aliens critique our Earthly food,
Saying, "Your pizza is rather crude!"
They prefer their meals in a cosmic stew,
And serve it hot with a side of blue.

Thus in a void, humor stays afloat,
While black holes find it hard to gloat.
For even the stars, with their twinkling light,
Crack jokes about life in the endless night.

Coastlines of Dreams and Wonder

On shores where giggles wash the sand,
Seagulls dance, not at all bland.
Waves take selfies with shells that glow,
As seaweed sways to a poppin' show.

Crabs in bowties throw a fancy feast,
While starfish joke with laughter, at least.
The ocean's laughter bubbles with glee,
A mermaid's wig floats by with a spree.

Jellyfish waltz in the evening tide,
With octopi guiding, they dance with pride.
The laughter echoes, splashes in play,
As moonbeams join for a night's ballet.

In these coastlines, dreams embark,
Where the fun begins, and makes its mark.
So grab a shell, and join the crew,
For laughter awaits, all shiny and new.

The Woven Tapestry of the Stars

In a cosmos bright with colors bold,
The stars weave tales of laughter untold.
With threads of light, they stitch the night,
Creating patterns that just feel right.

A clownish comet zooms past the sun,
Tickling planets just for fun.
Winking quasars laugh in delight,
As supernovae pop, oh, what a sight!

Galaxies twirl in a cosmic dance,
While black holes swirl in a giddy trance.
The universe giggles, twinkling wide,
As laughter echoes in the galactic tide.

So join the stars in this cosmic play,
Where humor reigns in a stellar way.
For in this tapestry, woven with cheer,
The universe smiles, inviting you near.

Secrets Drifting in the Ethereal Glow

In the glow of twilight, secrets abound,
Silly jokes drift, lost but found.
Fluttering whispers like butterflies sing,
Tickling fancies with every swing.

Dancing shadows play hide and seek,
Mischievous spirits, never meek.
They giggle at dreams that come and go,
As the stars join in on the soft hello.

Nebulas chuckle with puffs of glee,
Sharing laughs from a light-year spree.
Cosmic dust tickles the moon's bright grin,
As laughter spins wildly, deep from within.

So float along with these secrets afloat,
In the endless cosmos, let joy be your boat.
For in the ethereal glow, we find our place,
Where humor blossoms, a warm, tender grace.

Vibrations from the Celestial Depths

In the depths, a giant clam
Cartwheels through the cosmic jam.
Stars twirl in a dizzy dance,
While comets chuckle at their chance.

Purple moons throw a mock parade,
Jovial spirits in moonlight played.
Jellyfish juggle planetary pies,
As the universe erupts in sighs.

Giggles echo through the void,
Gravity's grip almost destroyed.
A rocket with a goofy grin,
Hurtles forward, let the fun begin!

Alien laughs in the misty air,
Spinning tales, goofy without a care.
Outer space, where mischief reigns,
Wonders sprout from silly gains.

Sculpted by the Solar Whispers

A statue made of sunbeam glaze,
Stands awkwardly, lost in a daze.
A breeze tickles its rigid nose,
It sneezes confetti, oh, how it shows!

Planets chuckle at its twitchy pose,
The solar winds tease with snickers and woes.
Round and round, it spins for kicks,
Twirling in space, just for the licks.

Meteor showers throw custard pies,
Old craters echo with muffled cries.
Starlight giggles at the uneven show,
As comets waltz and steal the flow.

Crafted by solar's playful shout,
This cosmic jester knows no doubt.
In the warmth of sun's quirky glow,
Laughter dances, silvery and slow.

Songs of the Shimmering Veil

Under the veil, a party sings,
Saturnian rings dance, make it swing.
A cosmic choir of shimmering glee,
Pleased to tickle the galaxy's knee.

Rhythm of stars, a baffling delight,
Shooting stars crash with glittery blight.
Celestial beings skip and hop,
As laughter echoes, they just can't stop.

A moonbeam plays the ukulele bright,
While asteroids join in a quirky fight.
Catchy tunes ripple through the night,
As black holes giggle in sheer delight.

With every note, the cosmos sways,
In a comic ballet of endless play.
Songs whispered from a thousand spheres,
Tickle our fancies and banish our fears.

Illuminations of the Titanian Night

In the night, the fireflies gleam,
Dancing to an outlandish theme.
With every blink, they tell a joke,
Tickling stars with every poke.

Saturn's rings wear goofy hats,
While extraterrestrial cats do acrobat hats.
They leap and prance in lunar light,
Making shadows dance in sheer delight.

Whispers of giggles float on by,
As space-time bends with silly sighs.
A comet rides a slinky dream,
Chasing laughter with a jubilant scream.

Underneath a quirky sky,
Galactic wonders flutter and sigh.
With each twinkle, a secret shared,
In the universe's fun, we all are prepared.

The Sea that Echoed Secrets

In the waves, fish traded jokes,
Lobsters wearing tiny cloaks.
The seaweed giggled, tickled foam,
As crabs danced far from home.

A dolphin dove with flair and grace,
Cracking puns in a splashy race.
Shells would snicker, pearls would grin,
As waves sang tales of joyful sin.

Scooters made from sea plants bright,
Seahorses zooming in sheer delight.
Even octopus joined the fun,
With eight hands, he's never outdone.

So if you hear the ocean's laugh,
Know it's a funny, fishy gaff.
Secrets ripple in bright sunlight,
In a world where humor takes flight.

The Forgotten Kingdoms of the Cold Moon

Once ruled by a walrus named Fred,
In a castle made of frost and bread.
Penguins in tuxes, quite the sight,
Held parties that lasted all night.

They served ice cream from snow-topped trees,
While snowflakes danced with every breeze.
A polar bear played the ukulele,
As seals wobbled, feeling quite zany.

But one day, Fred lost his crown,
Turned into a snowman with a frown.
The kingdoms laughed, but all was well,
For they built him a palace from gel.

So when the cold moon shines up high,
Remember Fred in his frosty sky.
With laughter echoing through the chill,
A kingdom where hearts are warm and shrill.

Narratives in the Misty Twilight

In misty fields where shadows blend,
A ghost named Chuck made quite the friend.
A squirrel who claimed he could fly,
But mostly just ate and asked 'Why?'

They spun stories of ancient trees,
Of haunted houses and buzzing bees.
The twilight chuckled, tickled bright,
As creatures roamed in soft moonlight.

A frog in a top hat croaked out rhymes,
While owls hooted punchlines through the pines.
The air was thick with giggles and glee,
In a realm where the quirky are free.

So if you wander in twilight's embrace,
Listen close for their playful race.
For stories float in the evening dew,
And laughter echoes, ever new.

Fragments of an Alien Heritage

Once landed on a bumpy rock,
Aliens danced around the clock.
With two left feet and goggle eyes,
They sang of Earthlings in disguise.

Their snacks were strange, a gooey mess,
An item that none could ever guess.
They nibbled on bright, glowing spores,
And laughed at their neighbors' silly roars.

A cactus spoke in quirky rhymes,
Sharing stories of interstellar crimes.
With laser beams and bubble gum,
The laughter echoed, oh so fun!

So remember this when you feel blue,
There's a galaxy full of giggles too.
For fragments of joy in space so wide,
Are treasures where we can all reside.

Fables from the Dawn of Shadows

In shadows cast by goofy trees,
A squirrel danced with wobbly knees.
He spun around, a sight to see,
While humming tunes like bumblebees.

A critter cried, "Oh look, a star!"
It was a glow-worm driving a car.
He took a trip on a jiggly road,
And left behind a twinkling load.

A rabbit laughed, quite out of breath,
As he imagined the glow-worm's death.
But near a pond, the fun began,
With frogs and fish joining the plan.

So if you roam where shadows play,
Just remember the antics that brightened the day.
For laughter hides in every nook,
In fables written in nature's book.

Chronicles of the Blue-lit Abyss

In the depths where the jellyfish glow,
A clam played music, stealing the show.
He bopped and swayed in a deep-water jam,
But forgot the beat, oh what a sham!

A fish with a hat thought it quite neat,
To join the clam's wildly offbeat.
They spun and twirled, a hilarious sight,
Under waves where the sun felt light.

An octopus donned a flashy gown,
And said, "Hey pals, it's time to clown!"
With eight silly legs, he danced away,
Creating laughter in the ocean fray.

So dive down deep, where the fun won't quit,
In the blue abyss where the creatures sit.
For every gurgle and bubbling cheer,
Tales of humor always draw near.

Epics Under the Glistening Canopy

Beneath a leaf where the raindrops giggle,
A little snail played a tune on a wiggle.
He sang to the bugs in a voice quite silly,
And made them laugh 'til their tummies got frilly.

In the branches hung a critter named Dave,
Who dressed in leaves and danced like a rave.
He tripped on a twig and fell with a thud,
But laughed it off, rolling in the mud.

A wise old owl perched up on high,
Said, "It's just fun when you laugh 'til you cry!"
And so the forest held a grand ball,
With twinkling lights and laughter for all.

Under glistening leaves, the jokes would soar,
As critters clapped and begged for more.
For every chuckle shared tonight,
Brings joy to the heart, it feels so right.

Writings from the Edge of Silence

On the edge where whispers meet the breeze,
A mouse was planning a heist with ease.
He plotted and schemed with a crumb for a prize,
But tripped on his tale, much to his surprise.

An old cat snoozed, dreaming of fish,
While the mouse laughed, thinking, "A close call, I wish!"

He tiptoed past with a wobbly heart,
As the cat let out a loud snore, like art.

In the stillness, a crow cawed just right,
"Your heist is a flop, you've lost your flight!"
The mouse giggled back, with an eye on the goal,
"For laughter is sweeter and makes me whole."

So in the silence where laughter ignites,
Tales twist and turn in the dimmest of nights.
A small little mouse finds joy in his chance,
And weaves through the darkness with his playful dance.

Letters from the Hollow Night

An alien writes with a quill of light,
Scribbles and giggles in the deep starry night.
With soup made of shadows, and a wink from the moon,
He sends silly notes, all filled with a tune.

His paper is stardust, his ink is the breeze,
He doodles odd creatures that dance in the trees.
A pickle-sized planet, he claims is his friend,
Together they giggle, and time they do spend.

The postman's a comet, so speedy and bright,
He delivers the laughter, igniting the night.
With chuckles like thunder, and jests soaring high,
The cosmos stands still, as they all laugh and sigh.

In letters of laughter, the universe beams,
Where silliness flows like a river of dreams.
From the hollow of night, the joy takes its flight,
In the quiet of space, they share endless delight.

The Icebound Lullaby of a Distant World

On a frozen moon, where penguins wear hats,
They skate and they slide, playful creatures—oh, bats!
With snowflakes like whispers, they twirl in the cold,
Each flake sings a story, absurdly bold.

The icebergs are grand, like castles in white,
Where snowmen hold court, dispensing pure light.
A snowball fight breaks, erupting with cheer,
While penguins all giggle, 'Let's freeze this year!'

With licorice lakes and hot cocoa skies,
The humor is thick and the laughter surely flies.
They wrap up their poems in blankets of frost,
Each line dripped with fun, never time ever lost.

A lullaby rises, soft music of snow,
Where winter's sweet chaos lets giggles just flow.
In this icebound kingdom, joy never fades,
As they dance through the meadows of chilly charades.

The Glimmering Voyage Beyond Reach

In a ship made of candy, they sail through the stars,
Jellybean sailors joke with grapefruit guitars.
Their compass is wobbly, their map's made of pies,
As they chase after giggles that float through the skies.

With clouds made of cotton, they nibble and chew,
While planets of pudding bounce shiny and new.
A cookie-shaped island appears in their sight,
'Let's dock here for fun'—oh, what a delight!

Their voyage is filled with strange sights to behold,
Like a cactus that dances and sings tales of gold.
With laughter erupting like confetti in space,
Every whimsy and wonder they chase with a grace.

In the glimmering glow of their shimmering dream,
They find all the treasures of friendship and cream.
Through mischief and marvels, they come back to teach,
That joy is the journey, and laughter's within reach.

Murmurs of the Cosmic Whisper

In a world spun from giggles, where shadows glow bright,

The whispers of cosmos bounce off into light.
With a wink from the sun and a twirl from the moon,
The stars blink and shimmer, they dance to a tune.

An octopus jester in zero-g spins,
With juggling of comets, let the laughter begin!
Galactic balloons float in colors so rare,
Each pop sends a chuckle through the vast empty air.

A grasshopper sings as he plays on his knees,
Each note is a bubble that climbs on the breeze.
'The universe giggles!' he hops with delight,
As the cosmos hums softly and twirls through the night.

In this tapestry woven with whispers of fun,
Where the echoes of laughter around us all run.
In the murmurs of space, where joy does not cease,
We find that in humor, our hearts find their peace.

Legends of the Icy Expanse

In a land where the ice does gleam,
A walrus is king, or so it would seem.
He wears a top hat, quite out of place,
Dancing in snow, with a smile on his face.

Penguins in tuxedos jump, twist, and twirl,
Chasing each other in a frosty swirl.
They slide down the slopes, squeaking with glee,
'Is that an igloo or just my knee?'

A seal plays the drums on an ice block tight,
While polar bears sing through the starry night.
The igloos are crowded, laughter fills the air,
Whispers of snowball fights bold and rare.

But the greatest legend is still untold,
Of a frozen pizza, that's worth more than gold.
It spun through the air, a cheesy delight,
Now it's the pizza that rules the night!

Glistening Dreams on the Twilight Coast

At dusk on the shore, a crab learns to skate,
With seashells for wheels, he's never late.
The seagulls dance, throwing glitter in flight,
While clams play the maracas, oh what a sight!

The waves start to whisper in rhythms so sweet,
About lobster ballads and shrimp taps their feet.
A dolphin named Fred joins in on the fun,
He spins in the air, 'This party's begun!'

The tide brings out treasures, like socks and a hat,
A pirate's lost plunder, but none are too fat.
'Yo ho!' shouts a fish with a beard made of kelp,
As the starfish applaud with a clap and a yelp.

The night lights up bright with the glow of the moon,
As the beach throws a bash — it's a shellfish festoon!
With beach ball confetti, laughter won't cease,
Such mirth on the coast, oh, what a wild piece!

Voyagers Across the Distant Ring

In a ship made of cheese, they sail through the stars,
Past Saturn's bright rings and Martian guitars.
An alien crew with googly, green eyes,
Shouts, 'Who stole the snacks? I'm not in disguise!'

The captain, a parrot, squawks loud and clear,
'Engage hyperdrive and shift into gear!'
But the engine just sputters, the radar goes wild,
As they drift through the cosmos, all tempered and riled.

A comet zooms by with a glittery tail,
'Is that a new ship or a very bright snail?'
They giggle and chuckle as they float through the void,
Making up games with their crew, quite overjoyed.

With asteroids dancing, it's fun all around,
They threw a wild party where no one was found.
In a galaxy filled with laughter and cheer,
They voyage forever, with nothing to fear!

Mythos of the Crystal Caverns

Deep in the caverns where crystals do shine,
Lived a gnome with a beard that was really divine.
He traded in gems, but mostly in jokes,
With voices of echoes that danced and provoked.

The bats played the banjo, oh how they did strum,
While goblins danced wildly and beat on a drum.
A troll tried his best to join in the song,
But he tripped on a crystal and tumbled along.

With laughter erupting, the caverns so bright,
The gnome spun some tales that lasted till night.
A treasure was hidden beneath a big rock,
But it turned out to be a big old sock!

In a world made of laughter, where mischief is gold,
The myths of the caverns are silly and bold.
With crystals and giggles, the wonders won't cease,
A laugh is the treasure that brings all the peace!

Whispers of the Saturnian Night

In the glow of a wobbly light,
A squirrel rides an orbiter, tight.
He claims he's a space explorer, you see,
Chasing asteroids, wild and free.

With a laugh that dances like stars,
He juggles satellites and old candy bars.
Each bounce on the rings makes him grin,
'Who needs a helmet? Let the fun begin!'

Comets zoom by, a playful race,
He twirls in joy, leaves not a trace.
Whispers of moons, a giggly tale,
As he chats with a space whale, oh hail!

In the end, it's a party of quirks,
With asteroids tapping out silly perks.
Underneath the snacks from afar,
The night echoes with laughter, bizarre.

Moonlit Chronicles of a Distant World

From a crater, a chicken takes flight,
Clucking her way through the radiant night.
She glows in the moonlight, oh what a sight,
Spinning stories of cosmic delight.

A llama in space boots joins in the fray,
Proposing a dance under Saturn's sway.
With moves that would summon a giggle or two,
They boogie for stars, a lively crew.

A cat with a cape leaps from a rock,
Saying, 'Time for my intergalactic talk!'
The aliens chuckle, they roll on the ground,
As they listen to tales of a cat's catnip mound.

In this realm where the planets align,
Every laughter breaks through the divine.
Chronicles swirl like candy in air,
As the night spins jokes, an endless affair.

Echoes of Frozen Lakes

Beneath the ice, a penguin sprawls,
Upside down, he answers space calls.
'my tuxedo's slick, but who needs to swim?
Let's skate on the surface, life on a whim!'

Close by, a fox in a fluffy suit,
Sips on a drink, a weird space fruit.
'The lakes here are frozen, but I'm quite warm,
Watch me do tricks; oh, you're in for a charm!'

As the ice cracks with a playful sound,
They dance in circles, round and round.
Frogs on stilts hop with elegant grace,
Making winter look like a real wild place.

In this land of giggles, the fun never fades,
With echoes of laughter that serenely cascades.
Each slip, each slide brings joy anew,
On frozen lakes, where the sky's always blue.

Dreams Beneath the Methane Clouds

Under thick clouds made of bubbly stew,
A frog in a top hat sings out his view.
'Why hop when you can float with ease?
Let's make a party in this cosmic breeze!'

He invites a raccoon with a shiny spoon,
Who stirs up the stars while crooning a tune.
The music's a mix of chuckles and glee,
As they dream of fables above the debris.

An octopus in shades joins the scene,
Twirling and swirling in colors unseen.
'Who needs solid ground when you have the air?
Let's dance with the sprites, without a care!'

Clouds flutter softly like candy on high,
Each puff a laugh, as they float by.
In their whimsical world, joy abounds,
As dreams bounce freely beneath strange sounds.

www.ingramcontent.com/pod-product-compliance
Lightning Source LLC
Chambersburg PA
CBHW071837160426
43209CB00003B/325